GW00319320

THE SPIRIT OF THE
EXMOOR PONY

LISA AND SHANAN LEIGH

HALSGROVE

First published in Great Britain in 2008

Excerpts from 'An Exmoor Lane' taken from *The Finish* (Halsgrove, 2001).
courtesy of the Trustees of Sir Alfred Munnings Art Museum

British Library Cataloguing-in-Publication Data
A CIP record for this title is available from the British Library

ISBN 978 1 84114 719 2

HALSGROVE
Halsgrove House
Ryelands Industrial Estate
Bagley Road, Wellington
Somerset TA21 9PZ
Tel: 01823 653777
Fax: 01823 216796
email: sales@halsgrove.com
website: www.halsgrove.com

Printed and bound by Grafiche Flaminia, Italy

Introduction

The Exmoor Pony has roamed freely for thousands of years and is thought to be the oldest type of British native pony. It is believed that they were first domesticated by the Celts.

All Exmoor Ponies are alike in colouring and markings. Their coat colour ranges from dark brown through to bay; all have the characteristic mealy muzzle. Exmoors

are hardy ponies, superbly adapted to their moorland environment.

Although all Exmoor Ponies have owners, the herds that wander the moors are able to fend for themselves, much as the Red Deer. In addition to these natural abilities, their foals can be tamed and enter into a life alongside people.

Once Exmoor Ponies were part of the workforce for a hill farmer, used for shepherding, hunting, transport and sometimes even ploughing. Those days have gone and their modern role is as riding and driving ponies in equestrian and leisure activities.

In the free life, the ability to solve
problems is part of surviving.
This has developed a keen
intelligence in the Exmoor Pony.

In terms of numbers actually breeding, the Exmoor
Pony used to be rarer than the Giant Panda.
However thanks to dedicated efforts
their numbers have recovered.

When days are hot,
they stand upon the hill
A silhouetted group against the sky,
With pricked up ears, bright eyes
and flowing mane.

An Exmoor Lane by Alfred Munnings

The Exmoor Pony Centre was officially opened on 26 July 2006, although its parent body, the Moorland Mousie Trust has been a registered charity since March 2000.

Unlike modern breeds, Exmoor Ponies are all very similar in appearance.

Wisdom that skirts the bog land, Courage that climbs the Tor.
Ponies for Islington by W.H Ogilvie

And in the spring the little foals are born
And there they all lie, basking in the heat
Of some gorse scented, blazing April morn.

An Exmoor Lane by Alfred Munnings

The raised flesh above and below the eye is referred to as the 'toad eye'. This is a protective feature that diverts water around the eyes.

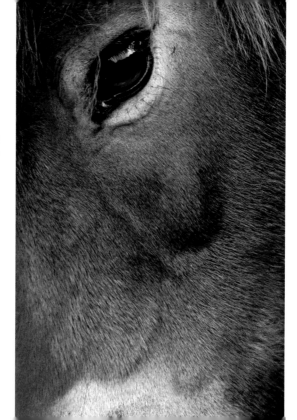

Their ancient ancestry has equipped the free-living
ponies with the instinct to flee if disturbed.

Exmoor Ponies, like all horses
and ponies, are sociable animals
and form friendships and family bonds.

The Exmoor Pony grows a coat in two layers providing thermal and waterproof protection against the harsh bleak Exmoor winters.

Although their breeding is planned by owners through choosing stallions, the moorland herds live an essentially wild life.

And as I watch them galloping away,
The rain and dying bracken all forgot,
I feel how weak am I, how strong are they,
Theirs is a life of freedom, mine is not.

An Exmoor Lane by Alfred Munnings

Evidence of the Exmoor Pony can be found in the Domesday Book.

The Exmoor Pony Centre works hard to
promote the use of this hardy
and versatile breed, and to achieve the
recognition the ponies deserve.

The older ones amongst
them seem to say
'You cannot stop us
coming up the lane,
for centuries we have
used this right of way'.

An Exmoor Lane
by Alfred Munnings

Exmoor Ponies have much to offer when treated
sensitively and trained with understanding.

The Exmoor Pony Society was formed in 1921 at the Lion Inn, Dulverton, to promote and encourage the breeding of pure bred Exmoor Ponies. The Society maintains the Exmoor Pony Stud Book and works to ensure the conservation of the breed.

The yearly roundup and check of the ponies is called the Gathering. The foals are inspected and assigned their individual number for identification.

Breed type: height is from 11.2hh – 13.2hh but more usually 12-12.2hh, neat small ears, the famous mealy muzzle, deep chest, small hard feet and low set tail.

In 1946 only about 50 Exmoor Ponies remained but thanks to dedicated breeders their numbers now stand at around 2800. Of these about 550 are actively bred from. 17% of the total live free.

The majority of Exmoor Ponies are indentified by their herd numbers/symbol and individual number branded on their near side. An unbranded pony may be registered but microchipped, or may be unregistered.

An Exmoor Pony can carry up to 12 stone in weight.

The Moorland Mousie Trust takes the surplus foals (particularly colt foals) from the yearly sales that would otherwise face an uncertain future at weaning and finds them foster or permanent homes before bringing them on as ridden ponies.